African-American

DEC 2006

LI

GRAPHIC BIOGRAPHIES

JACKIE ROBINSON

STORY:
KERRI O'HERN AND LUCIA RAATMA

ILLUSTRATIONS:
ALEX CAMPBELL AND ANTHONY SPAY

WORLD ALMANAC® LIBRARY

IN 1947, JACKIE ROBINSON BECAME THE FIRST BLACK BASEBALL PLAYER TO PLAY BIG-LEAGUE BASEBALL! AT THIS TIME IN THE UNITED STATES, BLACKS AND WHITES STILL DID NOT EVEN SIT NEXT TO EACH OTHER ON MOST BUSES. TO MANY AMERICANS, HAVING BLACKS AND WHITES PLAY TOGETHER ON A SPORTS TEAM WAS SHOCKING.

LONG BEFORE JACKIE ROBINSON WAS BORN, BLACK AMERICANS WERE FORCED TO WORK FOR NO PAY AS SLAVES. ALTHOUGH SLAVERY ENDED IN 1865, UNFAIR TREATMENT OF AFRICAN AMERICANS DID NOT. THEY WERE BARRED FROM MANY JOBS AND POORLY PAID IN THE JOBS THEY COULD GET. IN MANY TOWNS, THEY COULD NOT EAT AT ANY RESTAURANT OR LIVE IN ANY NEIGHBORHOOD.

DURING THE EARLY PART OF THE 1900S, BLACK AMERICANS COULD NOT EVEN PLAY PROFESSIONAL BASEBALL. FINALLY, IN 1920, BLACK BASEBALL PLAYERS STARTED UP THEIR OWN BASEBALL TEAMS, FORMING THE NEGRO LEAGUES.

JACKIE ROBINSON WAS BORN ON JANUARY 31, 1919, IN GEORGIA. HE WAS THE YOUNGEST OF FIVE CHILDREN IN A POOR FAMILY.

SAY "HELLO" TO YOUR NEW NEIGHBORHOOD, KIDS!

JACKIE'S TOYS

THE PART OF GEORGIA WHERE JACKIE'S FAMILY LIVED DID NOT HAVE MANY JOBS. SOON AFTER JACKIE WAS BORN, HIS MOTHER MOVED THE FAMILY TO PASADENA, CALIFORNIA. SHE HOPED FOR A BETTER LIFE FOR HER FAMILY.

HEY, BLACK BOY. GO BACK TO GEORGIA!

THE NEIGHBORS IN PASADENA TRIED TO FORCE THE ROBINSONS TO LEAVE. MANY WHITE CHILDREN CALLED JACKIE UGLY NAMES. THEY DID THIS BECAUSE HE WAS BLACK. JACKIE'S MOTHER, MALLIE, TAUGHT HER CHILDREN TO HELP EACH OTHER WHEN THIS HAPPENED. JACKIE'S BROTHERS AND SISTER BECAME HIS BEST FRIENDS.

BLACKS WERE ALLOWED AT THE LOCAL POOL IN PASADENA. BUT THEY COULD ONLY SWIM ONE DAY A WEEK.

BLACKS COULD GO TO THE LOCAL THEATER, TOO. BUT THEY COULD ONLY SIT IN THE BALCONY.

IN HIGH SCHOOL, JACKIE EXCELLED AT EVERY SPORT. HE RAN TRACK AND PLAYED FOOTBALL, BASKETBALL, AND BASEBALL. HIS OLDER BROTHERS ALWAYS ENCOURAGED HIM.

AFTER HIGH SCHOOL, JACKIE ATTENDED PASADENA JUNIOR COLLEGE AND PLAYED SPORTS. HIS TALENT CAUGHT THE EYE OF SOME COACHES. SEVERAL UNIVERSITIES OFFERED HIM SPORTS SCHOLARSHIPS IF HE PLAYED ON THEIR TEAMS.

JACKIE CHOSE THE UNIVERSITY OF CALIFORNIA AT LOS ANGELES (UCLA). HE STARRED IN BASKETBALL, BASEBALL, FOOTBALL, AND TRACK.

JACKIE HAD DREAMS OF "GOING PRO" AS AN ATHLETE. HE KNEW, HOWEVER, THAT PROFESSIONAL SPORTS HAD FEW OPENINGS FOR A BLACK ATHLETE. SO AFTER COLLEGE HE HAD TO FIND A JOB OUTSIDE OF SPORTS. HE WANTED TO HELP HIS MOTHER PAY HER BILLS.

IN 1942, THE UNITED STATES BEGAN FIGHTING IN WORLD WAR II. JACKIE ENTERED THE U.S. ARMY. HE HAD THE SKILLS AND AN EDUCATION BUT IN THOSE DAYS ONLY WHITE SOLDIERS BECAME OFFICERS. THE ARMY, LIKE THE REST OF AMERICA, WANTED TO KEEP BLACKS AND WHITES SEPARATE. SO THE ARMY REFUSED TO LET HIM ENTER OFFICER TRAINING SCHOOL.

OFFICERS CANDIDATE TRAINING

WE HAVE TO DO SOMETHING, JOE!

I'LL SEE WHAT I CAN DO, JACKIE!

A FAMOUS BOXER, JOE LOUIS, WAS IN THE ARMY WITH JACKIE. THE TWO MEN MET AND TALKED ABOUT THE UNFAIR TREATMENT OF BLACK SOLDIERS. JOE LEWIS SPOKE OUT ABOUT HOW BLACK SOLDIERS WERE BEING TREATED. BECAUSE JOE LOUIS WAS FAMOUS, MANY PEOPLE LISTENED. POLITICIANS IN WASHINGTON, D.C., HEARD THAT THE FAMOUS BOXER WAS UPSET ABOUT SEGREGATION IN THE ARMY. SOME POLITICIANS AGREED THAT THIS POLICY WAS UNFAIR. THEY PUSHED THE ARMY TO CHANGE. WITHIN A FEW WEEKS, THE "NO BLACK OFFICERS" POLICY WAS CHANGED.

SECOND LIEUTENANT ROBINSON REPORTING FOR DUTY, SIR!

JACKIE WAS PROUD TO FINALLY BECOME A U.S. ARMY OFFICER!

BETTER MOVE TO THE BACK, SOLDIER!

JACKIE FACED RACISM AS AN OFFICER, TOO. WHILE RIDING IN AN ARMY BUS, HE WAS TOLD TO MOVE TO THE BACK.

IN MUCH OF THE SOUTH, BLACKS HAD TO RIDE IN THE BACK OF THE BUS. BUT JACKIE BELIEVED THINGS SHOULD BE DIFFERENT IN THE ARMY. HE REFUSED TO MOVE!

THAT'S UNFAIR!

THE MILITARY POLICE ARRESTED HIM. LATER, THEY CLAIMED THAT JACKIE WAS DRUNK AND RUDE. JACKIE WENT TO COURT AND PROVED THAT THESE CHARGES WERE FALSE. JACKIE WAS UPSET ABOUT THIS TREATMENT. HE DECIDED TO LEAVE THE ARMY IN NOVEMBER 1944.

JACKIE STARTED THINKING ABOUT PLAYING BASEBALL. BUT HE KNEW THAT HE WOULD NEVER PLAY IN THE MAJOR LEAGUES BECAUSE HE WAS BLACK.

WHEN A FELLOW SOLDIER URGED JACKIE TO PLAY BASEBALL IN THE NEGRO LEAGUES, JACKIE JUMPED AT THE IDEA.

SOON HE WAS PLAYING FOR THE KANSAS CITY MONARCHS. HE EARNED $400 A MONTH. FINALLY, HE WAS ABLE TO HELP HIS MOM WITH MONEY.

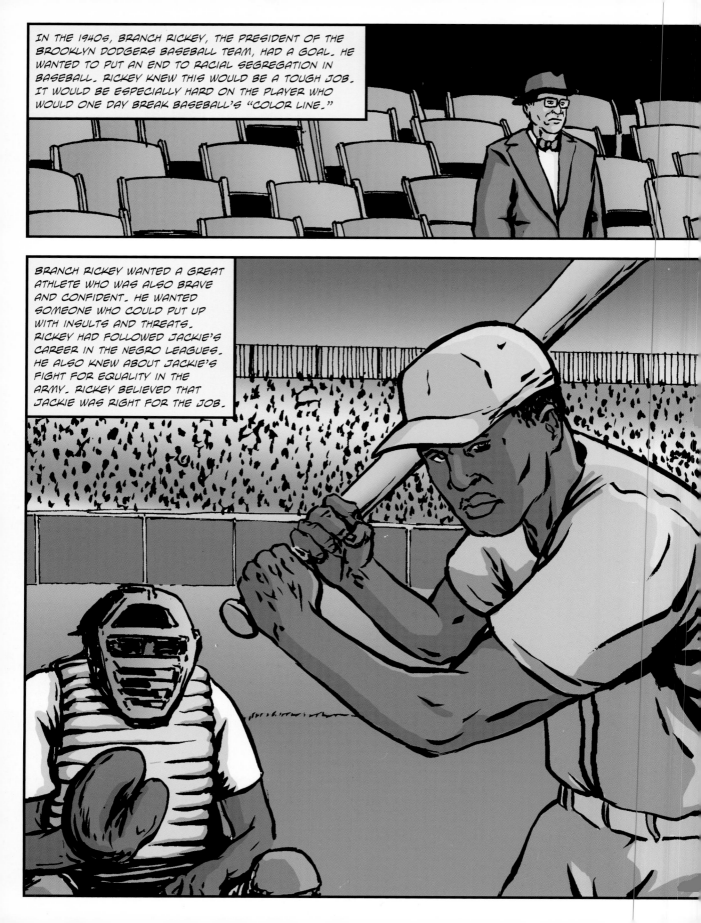

IN THE 1940s, BRANCH RICKEY, THE PRESIDENT OF THE BROOKLYN DODGERS BASEBALL TEAM, HAD A GOAL. HE WANTED TO PUT AN END TO RACIAL SEGREGATION IN BASEBALL. RICKEY KNEW THIS WOULD BE A TOUGH JOB. IT WOULD BE ESPECIALLY HARD ON THE PLAYER WHO WOULD ONE DAY BREAK BASEBALL'S "COLOR LINE."

BRANCH RICKEY WANTED A GREAT ATHLETE WHO WAS ALSO BRAVE AND CONFIDENT. HE WANTED SOMEONE WHO COULD PUT UP WITH INSULTS AND THREATS. RICKEY HAD FOLLOWED JACKIE'S CAREER IN THE NEGRO LEAGUES. HE ALSO KNEW ABOUT JACKIE'S FIGHT FOR EQUALITY IN THE ARMY. RICKEY BELIEVED THAT JACKIE WAS RIGHT FOR THE JOB.

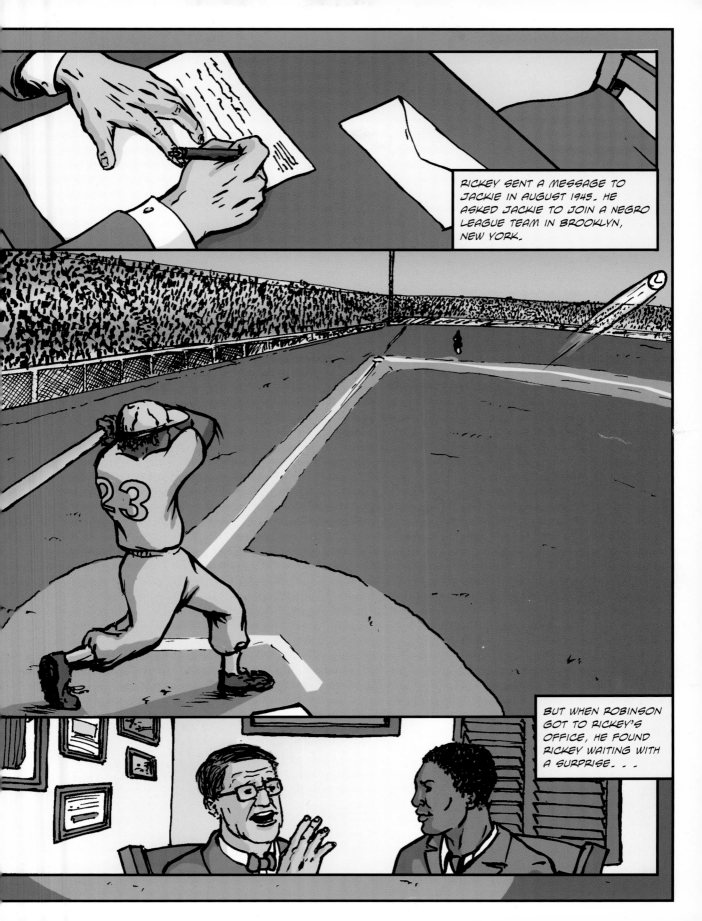

RICKEY SENT A MESSAGE TO JACKIE IN AUGUST 1945. HE ASKED JACKIE TO JOIN A NEGRO LEAGUE TEAM IN BROOKLYN, NEW YORK.

BUT WHEN ROBINSON GOT TO RICKEY'S OFFICE, HE FOUND RICKEY WAITING WITH A SURPRISE...

. . . RICKEY WANTED JACKIE TO PLAY ON AN ALL-WHITE MAJOR LEAGUE TEAM!

I THINK YOU CAN PLAY IN THE MAJOR LEAGUES. HOW DO YOU FEEL ABOUT IT?

LIKE MOST PRO BASEBALL PLAYERS, JACKIE NEEDED TO SPEND SOME TIME IN THE MINOR LEAGUES. RICKEY WANTED JACKIE TO START WITH BROOKLYN'S MINOR LEAGUE TEAM IN MONTREAL, CANADA. JACKIE WOULD MOVE LATER TO THE MAJOR LEAGUE TEAM, THE BROOKLYN DODGERS. BUT THERE WOULD BE MANY CHALLENGES, RICKY SAID. THE CROWDS MIGHT SHOUT INSULTS AT JACKIE. COULD HE KEEP HIS TEMPER UNDER CONTROL? EVEN IF SOMEONE HIT HIM, JACKIE COULD NOT FIGHT BACK.

THERE'S VIRTUALLY NOBODY ON OUR SIDE. . . AND I'M AFRAID THAT MANY FANS WILL BE HOSTILE. . . . WE CAN WIN ONLY IF WE CAN CONVINCE THE WORLD THAT I'M DOING THIS BECAUSE YOU'RE A GREAT BALLPLAYER AND A FINE GENTLEMAN.

RICKEY OFFERED JACKIE A CONTRACT TO PLAY IN MONTREAL FOR $600 A MONTH. JACKIE AGREED TO THE OFFER. HE ALSO AGREED TO TELL ONLY HIS MOM AND RACHEL ISUM, THE WOMAN HE HOPED TO MARRY.

THE WORLD LEARNED ABOUT ROBINSON'S CONTRACT SEVERAL MONTHS LATER, IN OCTOBER 1945. MANY REPORTERS BELIEVED THAT HE WOULD NEVER MAKE IT AS A MAJOR LEAGUE PLAYER. RICKEY HAD TOLD JACKIE TO EXPECT THIS AND BE PREPARED TO TAKE IT.

IN THE SPRING OF 1947, THE BROOKLYN DODGERS TRAINED IN CUBA. THEIR FARM TEAM, THE MONTREAL ROYALS, TRAINED WITH THEM. BLACKS AND WHITES HAD ALWAYS PLAYED BASEBALL TOGETHER IN CUBA. RICKEY HOPED THE CUBANS' TEAMWORK WOULD PREPARE THE DODGER PLAYERS FOR THEIR NEW TEAMMATE.

SOON AFTER SPRING TRAINING, RICKEY FELT THE TIME WAS RIGHT TO MOVE JACKIE UP TO THE BIG LEAGUES. HE HANDED REPORTERS A ONE-LINE STATEMENT . . .

Dodgers

"BROOKLYN ANNOUNCES THE PURCHASE OF THE CONTRACT OF JACK ROOSEVELT ROBINSON FROM MONTREAL."

THE BIG MOMENT HAD ARRIVED!

A WEEK LATER, JACKIE WAS WEARING NUMBER 42 FOR THE BROOKLYN DODGERS. HIS FIRST MAJOR LEAGUE GAME WAS APRIL 15, 1947, AT EBBETS FIELD IN BROOKLYN, NEW YORK. THE COLOR LINE IN BASEBALL WAS DOWN . . .

. . . BUT NOT OUT. ROBINSON ALMOST QUIT DURING THE FIRST SEASON. THE DODGERS WERE PLAYING A SERIES OF GAMES AGAINST THE PHILADELPHIA PHILLIES. THE PHILADELPHIA PLAYERS AND FANS WERE YELLING INSULTS.

THEY'RE WAITING FOR YOU IN THE JUNGLES, BLACK BOY!

WE DON'T WANT YOU HERE!

JACKIE TRIED TO STAY CALM. BY THE THIRD GAME, HE REALLY WANTED TO YELL BACK. BUT HE REMEMBERED HIS PROMISE AND KEPT SILENT.

YOU YELLOW-BELLIED COWARDS, WHY DON'T YOU PICK ON SOMEBODY WHO CAN ANSWER BACK!

FINALLY A DODGER TEAMMATE, EDDIE STANKY, GOT FED UP. HE YELLED AT THE PHILADELPHIA PLAYERS. AT LAST IT SEEMED THE TEAM WAS BEGINNING TO PULL TOGETHER BEHIND JACKIE!

FIRST BASEMAN JACKIE AND SHORTSTOP PEE WEE REESE, WHO WAS WHITE, MADE MANY FINE DOUBLE PLAYS TOGETHER. THIS RELATIONSHIP TURNED INTO A FRIENDSHIP.

ONE TIME, WHEN FANS WERE BEING MEAN TO JACKIE, REESE WALKED OVER AND PUT HIS ARM AROUND JACKIE'S SHOULDER. THIS SIMPLE GESTURE SHOWED EVERYONE THAT REESE LIKED JACKIE—AND THAT JACKIE'S SKIN COLOR MADE NO DIFFERENCE TO REESE.

JACKIE'S FRIENDSHIP WITH HIS TEAMMATES DID WONDERS FOR HIS GAME. THAT SEASON, HE LED THE LEAGUE IN BASES STOLEN AND RUNS SCORED.

THE BROOKLYN DODGERS WON THE NATIONAL LEAGUE PENNANT DURING JACKIE'S FIRST SEASON IN 1947. THEY FACED THE NEW YORK YANKEES IN THE WORLD SERIES THAT YEAR. THE YANKEES WON THE "SUBWAY SERIES" BETWEEN THESE TWO NEW YORK TEAMS. BUT THE DODGERS PLAYED WELL. THEY TOOK THE SERIES TO THE FULL SEVEN GAMES.

WAY TO GO!

JACKIE ROBINSON WAS NAMED THE NATIONAL LEAGUE ROOKIE OF THE YEAR IN 1947. BLACKS IN THE UNITED STATES SUDDENLY SAW JACKIE'S SUCCESS AS A RAY OF HOPE. HE HAD CROSSED THE COLOR LINE IN BASEBALL. THEY NOW HOPED THAT SEGREGATION COULD END IN EVERYDAY LIFE AS WELL. MANY BECAME HUGE BASEBALL FANS.

ROBINSON SPENT TWO YEARS BEING BRAVE—AND SILENT. FINALLY, IN 1949, THE DODGERS SAID HE COULD SPEAK MORE FREELY. AT MEETINGS WITH REPORTERS, HE TALKED ABOUT HIS FIRST SEASON IN BASEBALL. HE ALSO SPOKE AGAINST RACISM—NOT JUST IN SPORTS, BUT IN SCHOOLS, JOBS, AND EVERY OTHER PART OF AMERICAN LIFE.

I HAD STARTED THE SEASON AS A LONELY MAN. . . . I ENDED IT FEELING LIKE A MEMBER OF A SOLID TEAM. . . . THE DODGERS HAD LEARNED THAT IT'S NOT SKIN COLOR BUT TALENT AND ABILITY THAT COUNT.

AT THE END OF THE 1949 SEASON, JACKIE WAS VOTED THE NATIONAL LEAGUE MOST VALUABLE PLAYER! HE LED THE LEAGUE IN BATTING AVERAGE AND STOLEN BASES. HIS SALARY? A WHOPPING—FOR THEN— $35,000 A YEAR!

ACTION!

THE JACKIE ROBINSON STORY

JACKIE WENT TO HOLLYWOOD IN 1950 TO STAR AS HIMSELF IN THE JACKIE ROBINSON STORY. THE COLOR BARRIER WAS DOWN FOR GOOD. OTHER MAJOR LEAGUE TEAMS HAD SIGNED BLACK BALL PLAYERS. AND JACKIE WAS A NATIONAL CELEBRITY!

BUT EVEN IN 1950, THE FANS STILL HURLED INSULTS AT JACKIE. IN CINCINNATI, ROBINSON RECEIVED A DEATH THREAT. ONE WHITE TEAMMATE SUGGESTED THEY ALL WEAR NUMBER 42—TO CONFUSE THE ATTACKER!

JACKIE AND HIS WIFE HAD THEIR THIRD CHILD IN 1952. WITH A GROWING FAMILY, THE ROBINSONS BEGAN LOOKING FOR A LARGER HOME. BUT FINDING ONE IN ALL-WHITE NEIGHBORHOODS WAS STILL HARD. OWNERS WOULD RAISE THE SALE PRICE OR TAKE DOWN THEIR "FOR SALE" SIGNS. JACKIE'S FAME AND SKILL COULD NOT HELP HIM—EVEN IN NEW YORK, WHERE HE WAS KNOWN AND ADMIRED.

IN 1955, THE ROBINSONS MOVED TO STAMFORD, CONNECTICUT. FEW AFRICAN AMERICANS LIVED IN THIS SUBURB OF NEW YORK CITY. THE CHILDREN FELT UNCOMFORTABLE. JACKIE TOLD THEM THAT ONLY COURAGE COULD BRING ABOUT CHANGE.

JACKIE WAS A TRUE BASEBALL SUPERSTAR. BUT THERE WAS STILL ONE THING HE WANTED—TO WIN A WORLD SERIES. IN 1955, THE DODGERS FACED THE YANKEES AGAIN IN THE WORLD SERIES. THIS TIME, THE DODGERS WON!

YOU'RE GOING TO HAVE TO START TAKING IT EASY, JACKIE!

JACKIE KNEW HE COULD NOT PLAY BASEBALL FOREVER. BY 1956, HE WAS IN HIS LATE THIRTIES AND HAD HEALTH PROBLEMS.

ALSO, THE DODGERS HAD DECIDED TO MOVE TO LOS ANGELES. JACKIE DID NOT WANT TO UPROOT HIS FAMILY FROM THE EAST COAST. IN JANUARY 1957, JACKIE RETIRED FROM PLAYING BASEBALL.

IN JUNE 1972, JACKIE ATTENDED A CEREMONY AT DODGER STADIUM IN LOS ANGELES. THE DODGERS WANTED TO MARK THE TWENTY-FIFTH ANNIVERSARY OF THE SEASON WHEN JACKIE CROSSED THE "COLOR LINE" IN BASEBALL. THAT DAY, THE DODGERS RETIRED HIS FAMOUS NUMBER 42. IN 1997, IT WAS RETIRED FROM ALL OF MAJOR LEAGUE BASEBALL. NO PLAYER WOULD EVER WEAR ROBINSON'S NUMBER. NUMBER 42 WOULD BELONG TO JACKIE ROBINSON FOREVER!

A FEW MONTHS AFTER HIS TRIP TO LOS ANGELES, JACKIE ROBINSON DIED IN STAMFORD. THOUSANDS OF PEOPLE CAME TO HONOR THE MAN WHO HAD OPENED THE DOOR FOR BLACKS IN MAJOR LEAGUE BASEBALL. THEY ALSO CAME TO HONOR A MAN OF GREAT COURAGE. THEY CAME TO HONOR A MAN WHO, IN THE YEARS FOLLOWING HIS RETIREMENT, CONTINUED TO SPEAK OUT FOR RACIAL EQUALITY. THEY CAME TO HONOR A MAN WHO BROUGHT DIGNITY AND RESPECT TO A GAME, A PEOPLE, AND A NATION.

MORE BOOKS TO READ

Jackie Robinson. Crowell Biography (series). Kenneth Rudeen. (HarperCollins)

Jackie Robinson. Trailblazers of the Modern World (series). Lucia Raatma (World Almanac Library)

Jackie Robinson: Strong Inside and Out. Time for Kids Biographies (series). Editors of *Time for Kids*, with Denise Lewis Patrick (HarperCollins Children's Books)

The 1940s: From World War II to Jackie Robinson. Stephen Feinstein (Enslow Publishers)

Promises To Keep: How Jackie Robinson Changed America. Sharon Robinson (Scholastic)

WEB SITES

American Pioneers
www.sikids.com/news/blackhistorymonth/jackie.html

Biographies, Jackie Robinson
www.timeforkids.com/TFK/specials/articles/0,6709,714576,00.html

Heroes & Icons
www.time.com/time/time100/heroes/profile/robinson01.html

The Jackie Robinson Foundation
www.jackierobinson.org/

White House Dream Team: Jackie Roosevelt Robinson
www.whitehouse.gov/kids/dreamteam/jackierobinson.html

Please visit our web site at: www.worldalmaclibrary.com
For a free color catalog describing World Almanac® Library's list of high-quality books and multimedia programs, call 1-800-848-2928 (USA) or 1-800-387-3178 (Canada). World Almanac® Library's fax: (414) 332-3567.

Library of Congress Cataloging-in-Publication Data

O'Hern, Kerri.
    Jackie Robinson / Kerri O'Hern and Lucia Raatma.
        p. cm. — (Graphic biographies)
    Includes bibliographical references.
    ISBN 0-8368-6198-1 (lib. bdg.)
    ISBN 0-8368-6250-3 (softcover)
    1. Robinson, Jackie, 1919-1972—Juvenile literature. 2. Baseball players—United States—Biography—Juvenile literature. 3. African American baseball players—Biography—Juvenile literature. I. Raatma, Lucia. II. Title. III. Graphic biographies.
GV865.R6O32 2006
796.357092—dc22   2005027751

First published in 2006 by
World Almanac® Library
A Member of the WRC Media Family of Companies
330 West Olive Street, Suite 100
Milwaukee, WI 53212 USA

Copyright © 2006 by World Almanac® Library.

Produced by Design Press, a division of the
Savannah College of Art and Design
Design: Janice Shay and Maria Angela Rojas
Editing: Kerri O'Hern
Illustration: Pencils and inks by Alex Campbell, color by Anthony Spay
World Almanac® Library editorial direction: Mark Sachner and Valerie J. Weber
World Almanac® Library art direction: Tammy West

Printed in the United States of America

1 2 3 4 5 6 7 8 9 10 09 08 07 06